Mother's Memories

For my Son

Sons are the anchors of a mother's life.

SOPHOCLES

There is an enduring tenderness in the love of a mother to a son

that transcends all other affections of the heart.

WASHINGTON IRVING

Mother's Memories
For my Son

WRITTEN AND COMPILED BY DEBORAH NIXON

DESIGNED AND PHOTOGRAPHED BY ROBYN LATIMER

RAINCOAST BOOKS

Vancouver

For Kieran and all the other sweet boys

First published in Canada in 1998 by
Raincoast Books
9050 Shaughnessy Street
Vancouver, B.C.
V6P 6E5
(604) 323-7100
www.raincoast.com

Reprinted 2000

Canadian Cataloguing in Publication Data
Main entry under title:
Mother's memories : for my son

ISBN 1-55192-134-0

1. Mothers and sons – Quotations, maxims, etc. 2. Diaries (Blank-books)
CT9999.M674 1998   649'.132   C97-910860-8

Printed in Singapore by Tien Wah Press (Pte) Ltd

To: . . . .

With love from:

. . . .

CONTENTS

WHY THIS BOOK IS FOR YOU, MY SON

"That moment", the King went on, "
I shall never, never forget!"
"You will, though, "the Queen said,
"unless you make a memorandum of it."

LEWIS CARROLL

A LITTLE ABOUT ME, YOUR MOTHER...

My Names ....

....

Birthdate ....

....

Birthplace ....

....

....

Star sign ....

....

so that you may know me

[PHOTOGRAPH]

Who ran to help me when I fell,

And would some pretty story tell,

Or kiss the place to make it well,

My mother.

ANN TAYLOR

YOUR FAMILY TREE

YOUR MOTHER
Names

....

Birthdate

....

Birthplace

....

YOUR
GRANDMOTHER
Names

....

Birthdate

....

Birthplace

....

YOUR
GRANDFATHER
Names

....

Birthdate

....

Birthplace

....

*Your Grandmother's
Mother*

....

....

*Your Grandmother's
Father*

....

....

*Your Grandfather's
Father*

....

....

*Your Grandfather's
Mother*

....

....

*Your Grandmother's
GrandMother*

....

....

*Your Grandmother's
GrandFather*

....

....

*Your Grandfather's
GrandFather*

....

....

*Your Grandfather's
GrandMother*

....

....

YOUR FAMILY TREE

YOUR FATHER
Names

....

Birthdate

....

Birthplace

....

YOUR
GRANDMOTHER
Names

....

Birthdate

....

Birthplace

....

YOUR
GRANDFATHER
Names

....

Birthdate

....

Birthplace

....

*Your Grandmother's
Mother*

....

....

*Your Grandmother's
Father*

....

....

*Your Grandfather's
Father*

....

....

*Your Grandfather's
Mother*

....

....

*Your Grandmother's
GrandMother*

....

....

*Your Grandmother's
GrandFather*

....

....

*Your Grandfather's
GrandFather*

....

....

*Your Grandfather's
GrandMother*

....

....

Memories of my mother and father
(your grandmother and grandfather)

....

....

....

....

....

What you called your grandmother and grandfather

....

....

Memories of my grandparents

(your great grandparents) and other special people in my life

....

....

....

....

....

....

....

....

...The trees in the street are old trees used to living with people,

Family trees that remember your grandfather's name.

STEPHEN VINCENT BENET

FAMILY PICTURES

[P H O T O G R A P H]

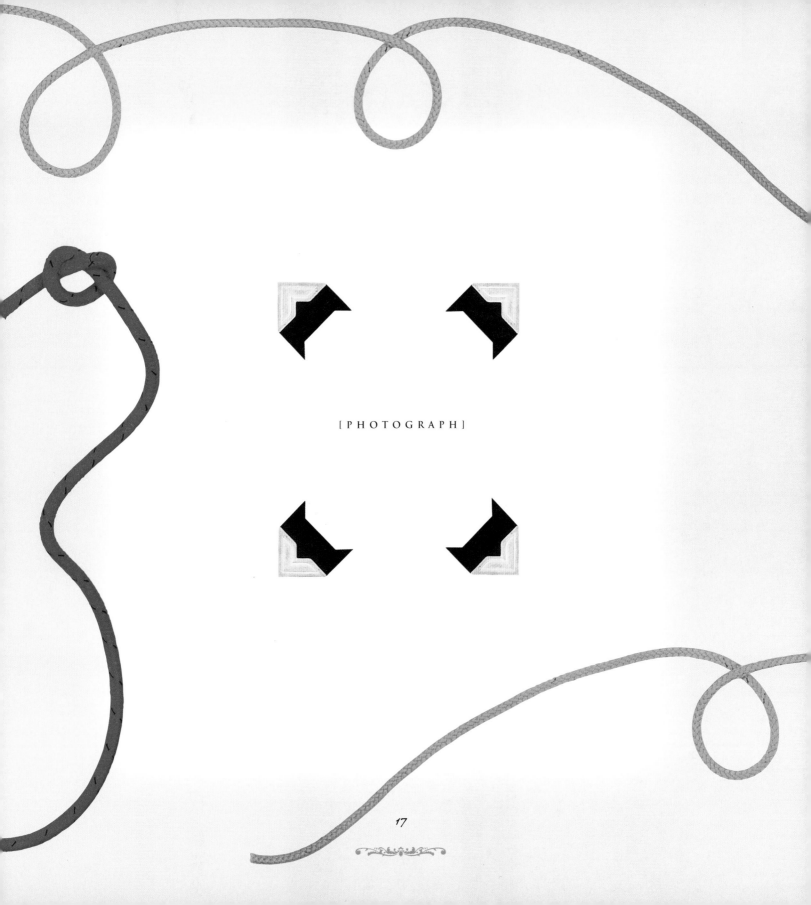

[PHOTOGRAPH]

My beginnings

My earliest memory

....

....

....

....

....

Where I grew up

....

....

....

....

....

WHEN I WAS YOUNG

My best recollections of childhood

The things I loved

BROTHERS, SISTERS, FRIENDS

What we did together

PHOTOGRAPHS

[PHOTOGRAPH]

My school days

My first school ....

....

My first school friend ....

....

How I got to school ....

....

Glimpses into how it was then ....

....

....

....

[P H O T O G R A P H]

[PHOTOGRAPH]

PLAYTIME THEN

My favorite toys ....

....

....

....

Games and schemes I remember ....

....

....

My dreams ....

....

....

WHERE I LIVED

My house

[PHOTOGRAPH]

....

....

....

....

....

....

....

....

....

....

....

MY ROOM

What I remember most about my room when I was young

....

....

....

....

More memories of my childhood

....

....

....

....

PETS

[PHOTOGRAPH]

[PHOTOGRAPH]

Pets' names

....

....

....

Pets' names

....

....

....

[PHOTOGRAPH]

[PHOTOGRAPH]

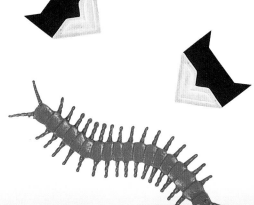

MY TEENAGE YEARS

BOYS

What we girls thought about boys

....

....

....

....

What I learnt that I would like to tell you

....

....

....

....

MILESTONES IN MY LIFE

My first kiss ....

....

....

My first job ....

....

....

My first trip ....

....

....

Other firsts ....

....

....

My first car ....

....

....

....

[PHOTOGRAPH]

STORIES FROM MY LIFE

....

....

....

....

....

....

....

PHOTOGRAPHS

[PHOTOGRAPH]

HOW LIFE WAS THEN

The fashions

Clothes ....

....

Shoes ....

....

Hairstyles ....

....

Cars ....

....

Fond memories
and special moments

Memorable times and unforgettable experiences

Formative influences in my life

People ....

....

Things ....

....

Places ....

....

Books ....

....

WHEN I MET YOUR FATHER

[PHOTOGRAPH]

40

The special things about your father

What attracted me to him

....

....

Recollections of our years together

....

....

....

....

Our first thoughts of you

....

....

....

OUR WEDDING

Date

....

Time

....

Place

....

[PHOTOGRAPH]

PHOTOGRAPHS

[PHOTOGRAPH]

WHEN I FOUND OUT ABOUT YOU

Evening star, you bring all things which the bright dawn has scattered: you bring the sheep, you bring the goat, you bring the child back to its mother.

SAPPHO

YOUR BIRTH

Your birth date ....

....

Time of birth ....

....

Your birthplace ....

....

Your star sign ....

....

....

Dear rose without a thorn,
Thy bud's the babe unborn:
First streak of a new morn.

ROBERT BROWNING

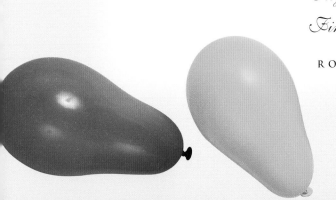

YOUR NAME

Names ....

What your names mean ....

....

....

Why we chose your names ....

....

....

What you might have been called

....

....

....

What everyone said about you

....

....

....

....

....

What you looked like as a baby

[PHOTOGRAPHS]

PHOTOGRAPHS

[PHOTOGRAPHS]

48

FIRST DAYS WITH YOU

Say, what is the spell, when her fledglings are cheeping,

That lures the bird home to her nest?

Or wakes the tired mother whose infant is weeping,

To cuddle and croon it to rest?

...For I'm sure it is nothing but Love!

LEWIS CARROLL

PHOTOGRAPHS

[PHOTOGRAPH]

[PHOTOGRAPH]

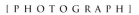

A babe in the house is a well-spring of pleasure.

MARTIN F. TUPPER

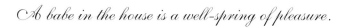

My thoughts when you came into my life

. . . .

. . . .

. . . .

. . . .

. . . .

Each mother's nurturing breast
Feeds a flower of bliss,
Beyond all blessing blest

ALGERNON CHARLES SWINBURNE

Of all the joys that brighten suffering earth,
What joy is welcom'd like a newborn child!

CAROLINE NORTON

YOUR FIRSTS

Your first smile ....

The first time you sat up ....

The first time you crawled ....

The first time you walked ....

WALKING AND TALKING

Your first steps ....

....

Your first words ....

....

Special phrases ....

....

....

EATING

Your first foods ....

....

Your favorite foods ....

....

....

....

SLEEPING

How you slept ....

....

....

....

....

....

Sweet dreams form a shade

O'er my lovely infant's head

Sweet dreams of pleasant streams

By happy silent moony beams.

WILLIAM BLAKE

PHOTOGRAPHS

[PHOTOGRAPH]

SONGS I SANG TO YOU

So shut your eyes while mother sings
Of wonderful sights that be,
And you shall see the beautiful things
As you rock on the misty sea
Where the old shoe rocked the fishermen three
Wynken,
Blynken,
And Nod.

EUGENE FIELD

SONGS YOU LOVED TO SING

Music you enjoyed

YOUR BEST-LOVED BOOKS

....

....

....

....

....

Other favorite things

....

....

....

Learn to read slow: all other graces
Will follow in their proper places.

WILLIAM WALKER

AS A BOY

Your early years

....

....

....

....

....

DAYS AT HOME

....

....

....

....

....

....

Home is where one starts from.

T.S. ELIOT

*They say there is no other
Can take the place of mother.*

GEORGE BERNARD SHAW

Things we enjoyed doing together

[PHOTOGRAPH]

YOUR FAVORITE GAMES

YOUR FAVORITE THINGS

Toys . . . .

. . . .

. . . .

Bears . . . .

. . . .

. . . .

Music . . . .

. . . .

Pastimes . . . .

. . . .

. . . .

YOUR FIRST DAY AT SCHOOL

. . . .

. . . .

. . . .

. . . .

Your teacher's name . . . .

. . . .

. . . .

Your friends' names . . . .

[P H O T O G R A P H]

. . . .

. . . .

YOUR SCHOOL DAYS

....

....

....

After school

....

....

....

....

Clubs and activities

....

....

....

....

GROWING UP

What I remember most about your growing years

....

....

....

....

....

How I felt as you grew

....

....

....

....

WHEN YOU WERE A TEENAGER

PHOTOGRAPHS AND CLIPPINGS

[P H O T O G R A P H]

From your childhood

[PHOTOGRAPH]

HOW SPECIAL YOU ARE TO ME

....

....

....

....

....

....

... a mother's love endures through all.

WASHINGTON IRVING

How life has changed for me since you came along

....

....

....

....

....

....

....

A dreary place would this earth be
Were there no little people in it;
The song of life would lose its mirth,
Were there no children to begin it.

J.G. WHITTIER

SPECIAL TIMES WITH YOU

[PHOTOGRAPH]

WORDS OF WISDOM

If a thing is worth doing, it is worth doing well.

Begin somewhere; you cannot build a reputation on what you intend to do.

Genius is immediate, but talent takes time.

Just because everyone else is doing it, doesn't make it right.

Do unto others as you would have them do unto you.

Gentleness and strength go hand in hand.

Mother knows best.

More words of wisdom

....

....

....

WORDS FROM YOUR FATHER

THE IMPORTANT THINGS FOR YOU TO REMEMBER

Qualities I would like you to have as a man

....

....

....

....

People to admire

....

....

....

....

....

WHAT I WISH FOR YOU

....

....

....

....

....

Remember there's no other

As dear, where'er you roam,

So don't forget your mother

And the dear old home!

ANDREW B. STERLING

Mothers are real people too.

ANON

[P H O T O G R A P H]